African Grey Parrots as Pets

A Complete African Grey Guide

African Grey Parrot facts & information including where to buy, health, diet, lifespan, types, breeding, fun facts and more!

By Lolly Brown

Foreword

The African Grey Parrot has a history that dates back to biblical times. It is one of the oldest species kept by humans for centuries! Its extraordinary beauty and an intelligent loving personality are what kept this parrot at the peak of popularity.

African Grey Parrots are gorgeous, playful and have the intelligence level of a six-year old with the temperament of a two-year old! Yes, they require serious commitment but are great lifelong companions.

Although this bird is a favorite among experts and bird enthusiasts alike, this is a bird that comes with a thick instruction manual to keep this amazing pet happy and healthy. In this book you'll be easily guided on understanding your grey parrot, their behaviors, their characteristics, how you should feed and care for them and a whole lot more.

Embark on the wonderful journey of sharing your life with an African Grey Parrot. Learn to maximize the great privilege of living with one and be able to share this unique and unforgettable experience just like the royalties that came before you!

Table of Contents

Chapter One: Introduction...1

   Glossary of Important Terms.................................3

Chapter Two: African Grey in Focus.......................2

   2.) Facts About African Greys..............................4

      Quick Facts 6

   3.) African Greys in History..................................7

Chapter Three: To Buy or Not to Buy?.................10

   3.) Ease and Cost of Care....................................13

      a.) Initial Costs 14

      b.) Monthly Costs 15

Chapter Four: Tips in Buying African Greys 18

   1.) Restrictions and Regulations in United States.............19

   2.) Permit in Great Britain and Australia 21

   3.) Practical Tips in Buying African Greys..........22

      a. How to Find an African Grey Breeder 23

      b. African Grey Breeders in the United States...............24

      c.) African Grey Breeders in Great Britain.....28

   3.) Selecting a Healthy African Grey 29

   1.) Habitat and Environment...............................31

      a.) Ideal Cage Size for African Greys.............31

      b.) Cage Maintenance.......................................31

2.) Diet and Feeding 36

   a.) Nutritional Needs of African Greys 37

   b.) Types of Food 37

   c.) Toxic Foods to Avoid 42

3.) Handling and Training African Grey 43

   a. Tips for Training Your African Grey 44

   b.) Trimming Your African Grey's Nails 46

1.) Basic African Grey Breeding Info 49

2.) The African Grey Breeding Process 50

Chapter Seven: Keeping African Grey Healthy 54

1.) Common Health Problems 55

Chapter Eight: African Grey Checklist 66

2.) Cage Set-up Guide 68

3.) Nutritional Information 69

4.) Breeding Tips 69

5.) Do's and Dont's 70

1. African Grey Cage Links 73

3. African Grey Diet and Food Links 77

Index 80

References 90

Chapter One: Introduction

At first glance, the African grey is a medium-sized, gray bird that looks like a pigeon, but further research revealed that it has a crimson tail, intelligent watchful eyes, and a stunning "hand-scalloped costume of armor" to its plumage.

These birds are also known as the "Einstein's" of the parrot world because of their incredible talking and mimicking ability which gave it quite a reputation among bird enthusiasts.

They are recognized in two distinct subspecies: the *Congo African grey* and the *Timneh African grey*. Both are found in—you guessed it—Africa!

So if you are thinking of getting one as a pet, are you willing to go to Africa? I told you, they're looking for commitments! But fear not! Thankfully there's another way for you to acquire these one-of-a-kind bird which we will tackle later on in this book.

According to animal experts, they do not actually recommend on getting an African Grey as your first bird. Buying a bird with this amount of intelligence and sensitivity takes a lot of thought before you undertake the responsibility of this parrot with a lifespan of possibly over 60 years!

It is not generally easy to care for as it will require tons of patience and understanding, which luckily you will all learn from this ultimate guide! Inside this book, you will find tons of helpful information on whether or not this is the right pet bird for you. Pet owners say that, *"once you own a grey, no other bird could ever satisfy you!"*

What a statement! To find out why this bird is truly extraordinary, read on!

Glossary of Important Terms

Avian – Pertaining to birds.

Avian Veterinarian – doctors who specialize in birds.

Beak – The mouth of a bird consisting of the upper and lower mandibles.

Breast – The chest of a bird located between the chin and the abdomen.

Breeding – an act of producing young animals

Brood – a group of young birds all born at the same time.

Chick – A newly hatched bird; a baby bird.

Clutch – The eggs laid by a female bird in a single setting.

Cuttlebone – the shell of a cuttlefish that is used for supplying cage birds with lime and salts.

Flock – A group of birds.

Gluconate – A salt of gluconic acid

Hatching – The process through which baby birds emerge from the egg.

Hatchling - A newly hatched chick.

Incubation – The act or process of keeping eggs warm which causes it to eventually hatch.

Mimicry – The activity or art of copying the behavior or speech of other people.

Nares – the openings of the bird's nose or nasal cavity.

Pinfeathers – a not fully developed feather emerging from the skin

Quarantine – period of time where the bird is kept away from other birds to prevent spread of disease.

Sexual Dimorphism – Referring to physical differences between the sexes of the same species.

Suppler – ability to bent or twist easily

Stargazing – a twisted back in birds.

Taxonomy – The classification of species into order, family, genera, etc.

Tetra-Chromic – four color light vision including ultraviolet.

Urates – a salt of uric acid.

UVA – a radiation that causes tanning of the skin.

UVB – a radiation that is responsible for sunburn in the skin.

Wingspan – distance from the tip of one wing of a bird to the tip of the other wing.

Chapter Two: African Grey in Focus

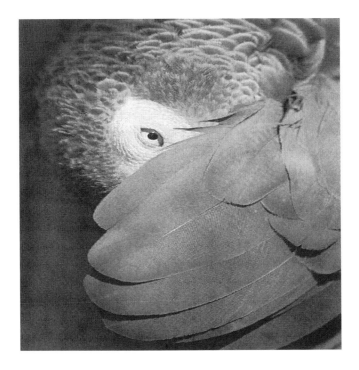

Before getting a pretty grey bird as your pet, it's very important that you know what it is inside out!

Like many other things, you need to have proper knowledge and invest a significant amount of time to truly study and understand where these birds are coming from. That is how you will determine if this kind of pet is the right choice, so that you know what you are dealing with.

1.) What Are African Greys?

The African Grey Parrot, which is scientifically known as *Psittacus Erithacus,* is a vulnerable species of Psittacidae. It is a medium-sized parrot and its distinctive features are its gray feathers with white markings around the eyes and black bleak.

There are two accepted subspecies - *Psittacus erithacus erithacus,* sometimes known as the red-tailed Congo African grey parrot, and *Psittacus erithacus timneh,* also known as the Timneh African grey parrot. The former is larger in size than the Timneh. The latter is smaller with dark-gray feathers and a chestnut tail.

The African grey parrot feeds on a variety of fruits, seeds and nuts, particularly those of the oil-palm. These birds inhabit savannas, coastal mangroves, woodland and edges of forest clearings in their West and Central Africa range.

These species is much appreciated as a pet, due to its high intelligence, sociability, ability to learn and reproduce human speech and its magnificent beauty.

2.) Facts About African Greys

In terms of geographic range, the two known species have varying ranges. Congo African grey parrot inhabits a range extending from Kenya to the eastern border of the Ivory Coast while the Timneh African grey parrot has a range from eastern border of Ivory Coast to Guinea-Bissau. They make their nests in tree holes and makes seasonal movements out of the driest part of the region in the dry season.

These parrots typically measure 33 cm from head to tail and weigh up to 407 grams. They have an average wingspan of 46 – 52 cm.

In terms of reproduction, the breeding season varies by locality but appears to coincide with the dry season.

They breed once to twice a year. Breeding occurs in loose colonies with each pair occupying its own tree. Females lay three to five roundish eggs, one each at intervals of two to five days. Incubation takes about thirty days and the young emerge from the nest at approximately twelve weeks old. Both parents care for their clutch of young until they reach independence.

In the wild, their average lifespan is 23 years, but in captivity, they last for forty five years, and can live up to sixty years! Now that's for keeps!

Wild African Grey parrots follow a daily pattern of vocalization; their impressive mimicry is also part of the fascinating facts about them, scientific studies have shown that they are able to make the connection mentally between words and their meanings, to express certain preferences and even to apply concepts such as color, shape and number.

These birds are mostly herbivores. Like what you have learned earlier in this book, they feed primarily on nuts and fruits such as oil- palm, and supplemented by leafy matter, as well as insects and flowers.

African Grey parrots are vulnerable to terrestrial predators which makes them a near threatened species. They are the most popular avian pet in United States, Europe and Middle East.

Quick Facts

- **Taxonomy**: phylum *Chordata*, class *Aves*, order *Psittaciformes*, family *Psittacidae*, Genus *Psittacus*, Species *Psittacus Erithacus*
- **Distribution**: Kenya, Ivory Coast, Guinea-Bissau, Sierra Leone, Ghana
- **Habitat**: Tropical; Terrestrial
- **Anatomical Adaptations**:
- **Eggs**: 3 to 5 eggs per season
- **Incubation Period**: 30 days
- **Average Size**: 33 cm from head to tail
- **Average Weight**: 407 grams
- **Wingspan**: 46 – 52 cm
- **Coloration**: White face patches, Grey contour feathers, black beaks, red tails, silvery yellow eyes
- **Sexual Dimorphism**: Males are slightly longer than females; Females have a narrower head and a suppler neck.
- **Diet**: nuts, fruits, seeds, insects, flowers
- **Vocalization**: mimicry; choruses
- **Lifespan**: 23 years in the wild; 45 to 60 years in captivity

3.) African Greys in History

African Grey parrots as pets are noted throughout history since the biblical times.

In the early 1500's it is said that King Henry VII of England had an African Grey parrot at Hampton Court. The wealthy nobility of Europe valued this pet for its attractiveness and intelligence.

According to Dr. W. T. Greene, one of the early authors of the 1800's, he believed that the African Grey parrot was actually known to the ancient Hebrews some 4,000 years ago. In the early days, the Portuguese seafarers called Grey parrot "Jaco" because it is related to the sound of their natural cry.

In 1774, German naturalist, Johann Bechstein described an African Grey parrot owned by Cardinal Ascanius. The cardinal's parrot was quite popular because it could recite the Apostle's Creed in an articulate manner.

The oldest surviving example of African Grey bird taxidermy can be found in Westminster Abbey in London. It was owned by Frances Teresa Stuart, Duchess of Lennox.

The most recent and significant research done was back in the 1970's by Dr. Irene Pepperberg of the Alex Foundation. She studied the intelligence and speaking ability of her African Grey parrot named Alex, who died in 1977.

4.) Types of African Grey Parrots

As you have already learned, there are two major types of African Grey Parrots. Take a closer look at this table and do a comparison to see which type you prefer.

Congo African Grey vs. Timneh African Grey

Congo African Grey	Timneh African Grey
• It's mostly Gray in color	• It's color is dark Charcoal Gray

• It is larger in size. It measures between 26 to 35 cm and weighs around 450 grams.	• It is smaller in size. It measures between 26 to 32.5 cm, less than the Congo grey and weighs between 300 to 400 grams.
• It has thick solid Black beak.	• It has Pinkish/ Horn colored beak.
• It has a bright Red tail.	• It has a dark Maroon colored tail.
• They are talented talkers and they begin talking between 12 and 18 months old.	• They begin to talk at approximately 6 months to a year.
• Feather plucking habit is very common among them.	• It has a less common habit of feather plucking.

Chapter Three: To Buy or Not to Buy?

After learning what an African Grey is, where they come from and how they live. This chapter will focus on giving you practical tips on what you need to know before buying one.

You will get a whole lot of information on its pros and cons, its average monthly costs as well as the things you need so that you will be well on your way to becoming a legitimate African Grey pet owner, should you decide to be one! It's up to you! Read on!

1.) *Pros and Cons of African Greys*

The information listed below is the advantages and disadvantages of owning an African Grey:

Pros

- **Personality:** They are loving, playful and highly intelligent
- **Appearance:** Has a beautifully crafted complexity
- **Noise:** Greys don't scream like other parrots, they only whistle, click and beep
- **Behavior:** They can be single birds, unlike other bird species, greys behaviors are highly individual.
- **Impact on Humans:** You will find yourself constantly learning about these creatures. It will be an educational experience for you!

Cons

- **Personality:** Quite sensitive, has a bit of temper, needs lots of attention compare to other birds.
- **Cost:** Price of the parrot ranges from $750 - $1,500 or more, it is quite expensive because it has better speaking skills than other bird species.

- **Damage to Your Home**: They like to chew things. Do not leave them out of the cage and unattended.
- **Behavior:** They do not like to cuddle; they do not appreciate intense physical contact. Just a few scratches will do!
- **Diet:** They need more calcium than any other birds.

2.) *African Greys Behavior with other pets*

Some bird species are very welcoming to other pets but with greys, not so much.

The Timneh may be more capable of accepting new family members than the Congo, but as with all birds, behavior is highly individual. Nevertheless, greys can learn to socialize and accept every member of the family. It depends largely on how you train it. Baby African greys often get along with other birds but if a mature grey is a first bird, it is more likely that it may not warm up to new birds unless they are carefully introduced.

Experts suggest that the best behaved grey parrots are those who were exposed to lots of change in the environment, noises and people because they become more adjusted.

3.) Ease and Cost of Care

Owning an African Grey parrot is more expensive than an average bird, so make sure that before you buy one, you can cover the necessary costs it entails.

In this section you will receive an overview of the expenses associated with purchasing and keeping a grey as a pet. If you cannot cover these costs, an African grey might not be the right pet for you.

a.) Initial Costs

The initial expenses associated with keeping African Grey as pets include the cost of the bird itself as well as the cage, cage accessories, toys, and grooming supplies.
You will find an overview of these costs below as well as the estimated total expense for keeping an African Grey:

Purchase Price: starts at $750 - $ 1,500

The price is generally higher for African grey parrots than the price for buying other types of parrots because of its ability to learn the nuances and intonation of human speech, which makes the prices of these parrots higher than other birds. It also depends on the size of the bird.

Cage: starts at $250 - $500

You will need a large, strong and secure cage. Cages of this size do not come cheap! You should buy something that preferably has lots of space suitable for cage play and activity.

Accessories: more or less $100 in total

You will also need cage accessories like perches, lights, feeding dishes, stands, cage covers and harnesses for your African Grey Parrot. Accessories can be quite expensive depending on the brand as well as the quality of your purchase.

Toys: average total cost is $50

As one of the most clever parrot species, your African Grey needs plenty of stimulation to keep their intelligent and active minds entertained. Keep birdie boredom at bay with chewable toys for your Grey parrot.

Grooming Supplies: more or less $70 in total

As part of pet hygiene, your feathered friend needs to be cleaned and properly groomed. There are lots of grooming supplies that you can buy online or in your local pet store.

Initial Cost for African Greys	
Cost Type	**Approximate Cost**
Purchase Price	$750 (£673)
Cage	$250 (£224)
Accessories	$100 (£89)
Toys	$50 (£45)
Grooming Supplies	$70 (£63)
Total	$1,220 (£1095)

b.) Monthly Costs

The monthly costs associated with keeping an African Grey is definitely not for cheapskates! Some of the things that needs to be bought on a monthly basis like food supplements, cleaning materials and even veterinary care every now and then will definitely add up to your expenses. Below are the estimate monthly costs it entails.

Bird Food: approximately $30-$40 per month

Your African Grey needs a varied and healthy diet. There's a massive selection of high quality seed diets, complete food and pelleted foods to choose from both online and in your local pet stores, as mentioned before, the cost will depend on the brand as well as the nutritional value of the food.

Feeding a variety of these foods, alongside fruits and vegetables is the key to a healthy parrot. If your African Grey is a fussy feeder, then buy supplements including vitamins and minerals in which you can add to either food or water.

Cleaning Supplies: at least $10 per month

You don't need brand new cleaning supplies every month, but of course, you will run out of bird shampoo and soap eventually. Just include it in your budget.

Veterinary Care: starts at $150 - $1,000 or more

Always take your grey to an avian vet for any medical treatment. Avian vets are trained specifically to work with exotic birds whereas a general practicing vet may not be familiar with their needs and treatments especially if they are sick, not to mention the medicines needed.

Additional Costs: at least $10 per month

In addition to all of these monthly costs you should plan for occasional extra costs like repairs to your grey cage, replacement toys, food supplements, medicines etc. You won't have to cover these costs every month but you should include it in your budget to be safe.

Monthly Costs for African Greys	
Cost Type	**Approximate Cost**
Bird Food	$30 (£27)
Cleaning Supplies	$10 (£8)
Veterinary Care	$150 (£135)
Additional Costs	$10 (£8)
Total	$200 (£179)

Chapter Four: Tips in Buying African Greys

If you are still interested in reading this chapter, that only means one thing: you have already decided to buy an African Grey!

Here you will learn tips and tricks on how to select a healthy grey, where to find the right breeder as well as the laws and permit you need to be aware of before buying.

1.) Restrictions and Regulations in United States

If you are planning to acquire an African Grey as your pet, then you have to think beyond the cage. There are certain restrictions and regulations that you need to be aware of, because it will not only serve as protection for your bird but also for you. Here are some things you need to know regarding the acquirement of African Grey both in United States and in Great Britain.

a.) What is CITES?

CITES stands for Convention on International Trade in Endangered Species of Wild Fauna and Flora. It protects the wild African Grey by regulating its import, export, and re-export through an international convention authorized through a licensing system.

It is also an international agreement, drafted by the International Union for Conservation of Nature (IUCN), which aims to ensure that the trade in specimens of wild animals and plants does not threaten their survival.

Different species are assigned in different appendix statuses such as Appendix I, II or III etc. These appendices indicate the level of threat to the current population of the bird with consideration to their likely ability to rebound in the wild with legal trade. The African grey is listed on Appendix I.

b.) What is a CITES Permit?

CITES imposes strict regulation on any species in Appendix I, which means that a permit is required to travel both to and from another country.

A CITES permit is a document that confirms you have acquired your African Grey through authorized channels and have not indulged the illegal pet trade that traps wild birds and exports them under horrific conditions in numbers that threaten their existence.

You must have a permit to leave your country; to enter another country; to leave that country and to re-enter your country otherwise it can lead to the confiscation of your bird.

The Division of Management Authority processes applications for CITES permits for the United States. You should allow at least 60 days for the review of your permit applications.

For more information on how to apply for a CITES permit please visit their website at: <http://www.fws.gov/international/cites/>

c.) What is the purpose of CITES?

The African Grey is one of the targets of illegal trapping and is usually hunted for profit.

CITES purpose is to encourage support and commitment to a unified cause. However it cannot enforce regulations in any nation, and does not replace their existing law, that is why some countries continue to legally harvest African Greys with no consideration to their dwindling numbers but since you are in U.S. you need to comply with the rules.

2.) Permit in Great Britain and Australia

In Great Britain and Australia you may need a permit for you to be able to import, export, or travel with your African Grey. This permit is called an Animal Movement License. It is required for the prevention of the spread of communicable diseases.

Like in the United States getting a permit is a very important thing you need to consider before you acquire a bird, because it is illegal to keep dangerous and endangered animals like an African Grey without legal permissions.

3.) Practical Tips in Buying African Greys

Now that you are already aware and have prior knowledge about the legal aspects of owning an African Grey parrot, the next step is purchasing one through a local pet store or a legitimate breeder.

Here are some recommendations for finding a reputable African Grey breeder in United States and in United Kingdom.

a. How to Find an African Grey Breeder

The first thing you need to do is to look for a legit avian breeder or pet store in your area that specializes in African greys.

You can also find great avian breeders online but you have to take into consideration the validity of the breeder. It is highly recommended that you see your new bird in person before buying anything on the internet. You can find several recommended list of grey breeder websites later in this book.

Spend as much time as you can with your prospective new grey before you buying. Interact with the bird and see how it is with you.

Continue the diet of the bird as advised by the store owner or breeder to maintain its eating habits. Look for any health problems or issues as well.

Finally, only purchase an African Grey that is banded. Banding means the bird have a small metal band on one of its legs placed at birth by the breeder which is inscribed with the bird's clutch number, date of birth and the breeder number.

Leg bands are indicators that the purchaser and the bird itself are in the country legally and have not been smuggled.

b. African Grey Breeders in the United States

Here are the lists of African Grey breeders in the United States sorted by state.

If you don't find anyone near you, contact the closest one to your location and ask for a referral or a lead of the trusted breeders.

Alabama
Admirable Birds

Alabama, Estill Fork: Tel. (256) 776-2120

Remarks: Does not ship; delivers within 200 miles of Huntsville, Alabama

California
Steven Garvin - The Feather Tree - www.feathert.com

P.O. Box 8401 Long Beach, CA 90808 - Tel. (562) 429-1892

Remarks: Free educational DVD with each pet bird. Please refer to www.feathert.com for availability, photos and pricing. They ships nationally.

Colorado
Rocky Mtn. Bird Farm and Pet Supply

www.parrots4ever.com

E-mail: www.rockymtnbirdfarm@hotmail.com

Monument, Colorado

Phone 719-466-3310 or 805-503-9592 - Fax 719-481-8273

Avalon Aviary Bird Store

6014 W US Hwy 34, Loveland, CO 80537,

www.avalonaviary.com

E-mail: avalonstore@frii.com

Tel. 970 663-5004,

Remarks: MAP-certified breeder

Florida

Ziggy's Avian Ranch

Hudson, FL

E-mail: bob.susan@verizon.net

Tel. 727-819-9839

Remarks: Will ship or drive 1/2 way in Florida.

Shady Pines Aviary

Royal Palm Beach, FL

Gloria Balaban

Tel. 352-454-4208

Jean (The African Queen) Pattison

New Tampa Highway, Lakeland, Florida 33815 U.S.A.

Phone: 863-686-4532

E-mail: afqueen@gate.net

Indiana
Royal Wings Aviary

www.royalwingsaviary.com.

Contact: Allan or Pam at (574) 273-1767

E-mail: pam@royalwingsaviary.com

Iowa
Zimmerman Pet's

N.W Iowa (Sioux City, IA).

Tel. 712-239-5531

New York
MY Lovely Doves and Etc.

Middletown NY 10940

E-mail: sheree@citlink.net

Tel: 845-341-0411

African Greys NY

www.africangreysny.com

E-mail: info@africangreysny.com

Tel. 646-737-2741 -

Remarks: They take deposits and ship

North Carolina
Avian Paradise - www.AvianParadise.com

Kernersville, North Carolina

Ohio

Parrotville Bird Shop, Brunswick

Oh 44212

www.parrotville.com

Tel. 330-273-0100

Oregon

The Parrot Patch Aviary

Eugene, Oregon

Tel. 541-463-9564

South Dakota

Feather Focus

www.featherfocus.com

E-mail: personal@featherfocus.com

Texas

SpringOak

Mailing Address: P.O. Box 231, Dripping Springs TX 78620

Tel. 512-630-1626

E-mail: Donray1953@msn.com

Utah

KCZAR Aviaries - www.kczaraviaries.com

Ogden, Utah

Tel. 801-731-5166

Virginia

Sissy Crawford - Sissy's Bird Colony

Aylett, Virginia

www.sissysbirdcolony.com

Washington

Jades Jungle Love

Arlington, Washington.

Tel. 425 238-4822

c.) African Grey Breeders in Great Britain

Here are the links to legit African Grey breeders in the United Kingdom:

Barrett Watson Parrots

<http://www.barrettwatsonparrots.co.uk/?p=african.greys>

Baby Greys UK

<http://www.babygreys.co.uk/>

Hand Reared Parrots

<http://www.handrearedparrots.co.uk/>

Xotic Birds

<http://www.xoticbirds.co.uk/>

Bird Trader

<http://www.birdtrader.co.uk/>

3.) Selecting a Healthy African Grey

African Greys can live for up to 45 years and more, these birds are long time companions, and its longevity depends on how your chosen breeders took care of them especially when they were just babies.

This section will give you simple tips on how you can spot a healthy grey that you can keep for life!

a.) Signs of a Healthy Bird

Look out for these signs so that you know if your prospect bird is healthy:

- The bird is perky, active and alert
- It should have bright and clear eyes
- It should appear well groomed with neat feathers.
- The feathers should be mostly smoothed to the body at rest - not continually fluffed.
- The feet and legs should be smooth and free of lumps, scabs and rough scales.
- The bird is healthy is when it's confident and inquisitive, although cautious and aware at the same time.

Chapter Five: Caring Guidelines for African Greys

Assuming that you have already bought an African Grey as your pet, the responsibility that comes with it is the most crucial part of the process. You as the owner, have to provide for its basic needs so that it will be healthy and happy. In this chapter you will learn practical tips as well as on how to properly care and handle your bird.

1.) Habitat and Environment

African greys need a clean, warm and mentally stimulating environment. As the owner you need to have knowledge of its habitat requirements and environmental conditions to ensure that your bird is healthy. In this section you will receive tons of information on the things you need to be aware of in order to create a great environment for your pet.

a.) Ideal Cage Size for African Greys

An iron parrot cage that is large and rust-free is the best home for a pet African grey. The ideal size of cage for an African Gray parrot is 2 feet deep by 3 feet wide by 4 feet high (61 x 91 x 122 cm). Never purchase a round cage. The basic rule of thumb is - the bigger the better!

The spacing between the bars of the cage should be no wider than ¾ of an inch. Of course, if the bars are too far apart, your grey might try to squeeze through them because they are naturally curious and they can get stuck. You don't want that right?

b.) Cage Maintenance

Your parrot's cage could affect the health of your pet so it's very important that you check it daily for any dirt, like the feces and spoiling food left in perches and cups to prevent health problems.

You should also change the cage paper every other day as well as check the metal parts & bars of your bird's cage periodically for chipped paint and rust, because your bird will most likely chew or swallow the flaked pieces. You should be able to clean the cage thoroughly at least once every month.

c.) Location of the Cage

After finding a cage you have to find the ideal place in your home as well. The cage should be placed in a fairly centered room, where there is interaction with people so that the bird will feel part of the flock.

The back of the cage should be located against a wall to provide security otherwise it will feel threatened and nervous if it is in direct traffic.

The cage should not be placed near the main entrance door of the house because it will feel threatened and nervous if it is in direct traffic and it would also feel disturbed and uncomfortable with new strangers.

d.) Recommended Supplies

Now that your cage is all set, you need to provide supplies to meet its needs. Here are the recommended supplies that your African Grey needs:

Perches

You will need at least 3 different perches such as wood dowel, natural branch type, a therapeutic perch or a cement perch. Having different types of perches will surely exercise the feet to prevent sores and foot related health issues.

Seeds and Pellet

You will need a good supply of packaged pellet diet, to be mixed with seed. Then you can slowly convert your bird's diet to a majority of pellet and fresh food.

Supplements

African Greys need more calcium than any other parrots. You should provide a good supplement such as cuttlebone, calcium treat or oyster shell. Avoid sugary treats like honey sticks and human junk food. Feed it treats like Nutriberries or Avi-Cakes.

Toys

You should purchase at least 3 different toys. It will allow you to interchange them in your grey's cage to prevent boredom. Sometimes everyone needs to have fun!

Dishes

Buy at least 3 sturdy dishes; one for fresh water, one for pellet or seed mix and one for fresh foods.

e.) Grooming and Hygiene

Here are some things you need to know on how to maintain your bird's hygiene and keep a healthy life.

Provide a misting bottle or a birdbath. All birds should be gently misted with a water bottle. Never spray the bird directly in its face.

It's important that you keep an eye in your bird while it is bathing. Bathe your grey often with clean water. Distilled water is sometimes required. Speak to your veterinarian on the best choice of water for your bird. During its misting and bathing procedures, make sure there are no drafts because it can cause respiratory issues. It may chill your bird when he is wet. Use towels and blankets, but be careful because it can catch the bird's nails and beaks in their threads.

To ensure that the oils from their skin glands, disease organisms or items such as lotions and hand creams do not transfer to your bird's feathers, wash your hands with soap and water thoroughly before handling your grey.

Your bird may be ill if it seems to stop grooming and becomes dirty. Once you see this signs, contact your avian veterinarian immediately.

f.) Lighting and Temperature

Your average room temperature for your bird should not exceed 80 degrees. Avoid drafty areas that will get direct heat from sun for any portion of the day.

Parrots also have tetra-chromic vision (4 color light vision including ultraviolet), that's why a full color light bulb must be present in the cage area. The incandescent or monochromatic light bulbs usually found in households are not a good choice for your bird.

Cover the cage during nighttime; it blocks out any excess light and also creates a more secure sleeping place. Be careful when using fabrics as cover because your bird might rip it with its claws or beak and could likely eat it.

Never ever place the cage in the kitchen or somewhere near cooking fumes because greys are very sensitive, that even a small amount of smoke can be fatal.

2.) Diet and Feeding

African Grey parrots are largely considered omnivorous due to lack of fixed food preferences. Its food preferences are mostly based on its natural habitat. Thankfully, today's supplements have opened new and healthy options for pet owners. In this section you will be guided on how to properly feed your parrot and learn the nutritional requirements they need.

a.) Nutritional Needs of African Greys

Contrary to popular belief, birds do not live by seed alone! A seed only diet can be extremely dangerous because it can result in nutrient deficiency and diseases due to its limited nutrients, vitamins and minerals which could shorten the life expectancy of your parrot. Greys need a good quality pellet diet for it to be healthy. Like humans, parrots need a balanced diet. You should be able to feed your bird with fresh vegetables especially green leafy ones as well as fruit and grain daily.

This section outlines the foods your pet will appreciate in order to meet the majority of its dietary needs.

b.) Types of Food

Seeds

African Grey Parrots love to eat seeds! Palm fruit seeds are highly recommended on a Grey parrot's diet plan. However as mentioned earlier, you still need to offer a proper balance of fruits and vegetables because that will keep the bird's metabolic system strong.

African greys need 3-4 teaspoons per day of a pellet or seed-based, fortified parrot diet.

Fresh Vegetables

Vegetables are a rich source of natural fiber for the body. As compared to other birds, there are a few vegetables which is essential for an African Grey, these vegetables not only provide fiber but also nutrition.

Just make sure they are properly washed before feeding to your pet.

Below is the list of highly recommended vegetables for African Greys:

- **Sweet Potato** – can be served in the cooked and mashed form.
- **Carrots** – can be served in the boiled form
- **Peppers** – green, red, and yellow betters are high in vitamin C, which is essential for the bird's immune system.
- **Spinach, Broccoli and Cauliflower** – can be consumed raw or cooked.
- **Yellow and Butter nut squashes**
- **Kale**
- **Celery**
- **Cucumbers**
- **Green beans**
- **Peas – garden and snow**
- **Leaf lettuce (not head or iceberg lettuce)**

Fruits

Fruits are healthy and sweet, they are a natural source of sugars for the parrots. Below are list of fruits that are highly recommended by veterinarians.

Keep in mind that you need to get your vet's approval before trying a new fruit for your African Grey Parrot.

- Melons
- Dried dates
- Figs
- Gooseberries
- Mango and Papaya (with skins removed)
- Grapes
- Guava
- Honeydew
- Kiwi
- Apples
- Banana
- Blackcurrant
- Blueberry
- Cantaloupe
- Cherry
- Mango
- Pear
- Pineapple
- Pomegranate

- Raspberry
- Strawberry

Important Reminder:

About 5-10% of an African grey's diet should be bite-sized. Offer fruits and vegetables daily or every 2-3 days.

Supplements

The only supplement necessary in feeding your parrot is Calcium. As mentioned before, grey birds need the most amount of Calcium than any other kinds of parrots.

Calcium is usually found in the form of a cuttlebone or Calcium treat that is attached inside your bird cage. You can also offer a powdered supplement such as packaged oyster shell which can be added directly to your pet's food. Follow the instructions on the supplement package. Calcium is vital for muscle contraction, blood clotting, heart functions, bone growth and strength.

The bird should be exposed to UVB light for at least 3-4 hours a day, for optimal physiologic use of the calcium you are giving your bird.

Vitamins

Vitamin is definitely an important part of any diet because it fulfills body requirements but as a precaution most Grey parrots on a pelleted diet do not require additional vitamins therefore a regular medical consultation to your veterinary is highly advised to ensure that your bird is getting proper diet. Some Greys are prone to vitamin A deficiencies but you should not provide vitamins without an expert's prescription.

Fatty Acids

Fatty acids are part of a balanced diet combined with minerals, vitamins and calcium. Fatty acid intake serves as an effective skin and feather care agent. It also provides the ability to develop a better immune system so that it may survive possible common diseases among the bird family. It also plays an important role in reducing the risk of heart attacks as well as lowering the cholesterol level.

Important Reminder

Vitamins and mineral supplement may be mixed with fruits and veggies at least once a week or as prescribed by the veterinarian.

Water

Hydration is just as important for birds as it is for human beings especially during hot weather conditions, lack of water can lead to dehydration which can cause these birds to collapse. Your African Greys should be given access to clean, fresh and cool water. Do not use tap water because can cause the bird to be ill, as well as distilled water, instead use unflavored bottled drinking water or bottled natural spring water. If in case, tap water is used, treat it with a de-chlorinating treatment. Inability to provide fresh water to pet birds can cause upset stomach with unbearable stomachache.

Whether the meal consists of raw or cooked food, vegetables or meat African Greys have a habit of drinking water after every meal which helps their digestion process.

All water given to birds for drinking, as well as water used for misting, soaking or bathing must be 100% free of chlorine and heavy metals.

c.) Toxic Foods to Avoid

Some foods are specifically toxic for your African Grey Parrot. Make sure that your bird never gets to eat one of the toxic items below and ensure that an avian veterinary checks your bird every now and then. These harmful foods is as important as selecting the right supplements and food items for your bird.

The following list of plants, fruits and beans are toxic for African Grey Parrots:

- Avocado
- Azalea
- Baneberry

- Beans: (Castor, Horse, Fava, Broad, Glory, Scarlet Runner, Mescal, Navy and Pregatory)
- Coffee (Senna)
- Coffee Bean (Rattle bush, Rattle Box & Coffee weed)
- Eucalyptus (Dried, Dyed Or Treated in floral arrangements)
- Grass: (Johnson, Sorghum, Sudan & Broom Corn)
- Hyacinth
- Marijuana (Hemp)
- Oak
- Red Maple
- Tobacco
- Umbrella Plant
- White Cedar, China
- Berry
- Yellow Jasmine

3.) Handling and Training African Grey

There would be instances that your pet will be out of its cage; after all, what's the point of its beauty and intelligence if you won't let it fly right? However, it's also important to keep in mind on how to properly handle and train your Grey bird so that it will not cause harm to itself and to people as well.

In this section, you'll learn some guidelines on how to confidently handle your parrot as well as some tips on trimming its nails and wings to maximize its balance and flying potential.

a. Tips for Training Your African Grey

Training an African Grey is not that hard to do, in fact it can be a fun and rewarding bonding experience for you and your feathered friend! Unlike any other bird, your Grey's level of comprehension allows it to relatively absorb information very quickly and easily.

Trust is the most important key in training your parrot. The first thing you need to do is to be able to establish a solid connection and rapport between you and your pet.

This section will provide some guidelines you can follow in getting your bird to sit still through training sessions like a five-year-old child! Are you ready? Read on!

Despite of the African Grey's cleverness, the flip side is that they can be mischievous and they tend to get bored easily. Spend only about a maximum of 10 to 15 minutes per session and never allow yourself to go over this specific time limit; otherwise your African Grey's attention span may begin to wane and it will get tired.

When you've gotten your African Grey out of your cage, allow the bird to warm up first. One of the first lessons you could teach is how to flap its wings because it is natural to them and therefore easier to do.

For your bird to be able to flap its wings, you need to do a maneuver called the "earthquake." While the parrot is perched on your hand, ensure that it has a good grip on your fingers, and then suddenly lower your arm. This maneuver will cause the parrot to flap its wings to regain its balance.

The next thing you can do is practice some wordplay. Say words like "flap" so that your parrot can begin to comprehend what is expected of him when you say "flap", and of course always give him a treat. Positive reinforcement is more effective than negative because it might confuse the parrot and also cause bad attitude.

Now, if an African Grey has already understood the difference between the words "yes" and "no," you can use it to stop a certain behavior. Just tell him "no" very firmly, African Greys are intelligent enough to deduce the difference.

Ensure that there are no distractions during a training session, like a five-year old, their attention span is very short, so you want to keep your bird's attention fully on you. It's also best to keep your voice loud and clear, if ever other people are watching this will teach the African Grey on which voice he has to respond to and hopefully that is yours.

b.) Trimming Your African Grey's Nails

Like many parrots, African Greys have a very sharp, needle-like nails because they do a lot of climbing in the wild, and they also use these nails to dig into wood to keep them secure.

Unclipped nails can dig into the skin, leaving scratches or painful wounds to a person, only clipped to a point that the bird can perch securely and does not bother you when the bird is perched on your hand. Many people have their grey's nails clipped to the point that it becomes dull and the bird can no longer grip a perch firmly. This can result to becoming more clumsy and nervous because it cannot move without slipping. This nervousness can develop into fear biting and panic attacks.

Another tip is only use a styptic powder on your bird's nails, not the skin!

c.) Clipping an African Grey's Wings

We all know that birds are supposed to fly especially for a young African grey. Greys can be fairly clumsy and flying gives them confidence as well as agility, stamina, and muscle tone.

Consult a qualified veterinarian to show you the proper way in clipping a bird's wings. A certain amount of flight feathers will be removed while leaving the smaller balancing feathers inside the wing closer to the body uncut.

It is also recommended that if your grey is a baby (only few months old), you should hold off on its first clipping until it is fully capable of flight and has developed confidence.

Chapter Six: Breeding African Greys

If you decided to buy two African Greys, for instance a male and female and keep them together, you should definitely prepare for the possibility of breeding, unless it's the same gender, otherwise you're going to be caught off guard!

If you are interested in breeding your African Greys this chapter will give you a wealth of information about the processes and phases of its breeding and you will also learn how to properly breed African Greys on your own. This is not for everyone but if you want to have better understanding about how these birds come about, then you should definitely not miss this part! On the contrary if you are interested in becoming a reputable breeder, then this is a must read chapter for you.

1.) Basic African Grey Breeding Info

Before deciding if you truly want to become a breeder, you should at least have prior knowledge on their basic reproduction process and behavior. This section will inform you on how these creatures procreate.

a.) Sexual Dimorphism

There is no sexual dimorphism with African Greys. This is one of the things that set these parrots apart from other kinds of birds. Both the gender of African Grey Parrot is visually identical. You can only determine it through DNA analysis, which uses sample blood or feathers. Although, some breeders claim that they can distinguish if the bird is male or female because of its features, it is still indefinite unless it's DNA is tested.

It can also provide additional information on its sexual maturity and capability to reproduce. It is inexpensive and convenient so if you like to know more about your bird's sexuality you should definitely try DNA Sexing or Surgical Sexing.

b.) Mating and Reproduction

African Greys like other parrots will mate often. The male will mount over the female and copulate. This usually takes place between midnight and around four o'clock in the morning. They mate for almost 20 minutes and their feed intake increases during this period.

After one month since the first mating, female greys lay 4-5 eggs with a gap of 2-3 days between each egg and they spent most of the time in the cage.

2.) The African Grey Breeding Process

In order to have a clear sketch of African Grey parrot breeding, this section will show you the breeding process and the information you need to know, so that your pets can successfully procreate.

a.) Selecting African Grey parrots for Breeding

For you to select a healthy, fertile and active parrot it is recommended that your parrot undergoes clinical examination by a veterinarian. This is essential to determine if your parrot is capable of reproduction or not and at the same time it can prevent diseases that could be transmitted to the coming flock.

b.) Selection of a Good Pair

It is important that you choose a pair that can reproduce and lay fertile healthy eggs. Although this is not totally under your control but the better the selected breeding pair, the better will be the progeny.

The female African Grey Parrot is very choosy when it comes to selecting its mate. It prefers to choose a male with the biggest crop, so that male parrot can feed the chicks. Male parrots sing and show off to attract a female.

Try at least 5-6 pairs so that you can observe the bonding of different couples. If you already bought a male and female and it is in good condition, then you will have no problem, because they already found its mate.

c.) Setting up a Good Environment and Cage

In the wild, African Grey Parrots are usually cavity dwellers. They do not build a nest, but lay their eggs in cavities found in trees. In captivity, you need to set up a nice environment (preferably something that looks like a natural forest), and a nest in the cage. The ideal dimensions of a cage for breeding are 2 feet width, 3 feet high & 6 feet deep.

Set up an L shaped nest that measures 2 feet high and two feet deep at the base, because in the wild, African Grey females make an L shape nest with a hole at the top to enter and leave. Also add some peat, wood chips, and small pieces of coconut fibers, foam, dry grass or hay to the bottom of the nest. Put your cage at a place where they will feel secure and where nobody will disturb them.

d.) Brooding and Incubation

The brooding time starts after laying 4-5 eggs, and the incubation period is almost 28-30 days from the day the female laid the last egg. Female greys only leave the nest in the morning or late at night to get a drink and to defecate.

e.) Hatching

After 28-30 days the eggs hatch and a new baby African Grey comes out of the shell. The parents spent a large amount of food during this period because they have to feed the young ones too.

Chapter Seven: Keeping African Grey Healthy

You as the owner should be aware of the potential threats and diseases that could harm the wellness of your African Grey. Just like human beings, you need to have knowledge on these diseases so that you can prevent it from happening in the first place. You will find tons of information on the most common problems that may affect your bird including its causes, signs and symptoms, remedies and prevention.

1.) Common Health Problems

In this section, you will learn about the diseases that may affect and threaten your Grey's wellness. Learning these diseases as well as its remedies is vital for you and your bird so that you could prevent it from happening or even help with its treatment in case they caught one.

Below are some of the most common health problems that occur specifically to African Grey parrots. You will learn some guidelines on how these diseases can be prevented and treated as well as its signs and symptoms.

Hypocalcaemia (Low Calcium)

Hypocalcaemia syndrome is associated with low calcium levels in the blood, which can cause seizures. Baby African Greys aged 2 to 5 are most commonly affected.

a.) Cause of Hypocalcaemia

The main cause of low calcium is limited access to natural sunlight such as in the northern hemisphere during the winter months; full-spectrum lamps can be used to provide UVA and UVB rays.

b.) Signs and Symptoms

Here are the signs that your pet might be lacking in Calcium:

- Weak immune systems; susceptibility to diseases

- Soft bones; bent keels, splayed legs

- Abnormal beak development

- Reproductive problems (egg binding, soft-shell eggs, dying chicks)

- Seizures

- Stargazing (twisted back)

c.) Treatment

Grey parrots suffering from seizures are often treated with intravenous calcium gluconate, as well as with diazepam, but consult with your veterinarian first for prescription.

d.) Prevention

Health problems associated with low calcium levels can be prevented by providing sufficient access to natural sunlight to your bird. Vitamin D is necessary for bone health. The sunlight is utilized by your bird's feathers, which will undergo a chemical reaction producing

Vitamin D3 and the bird ingest it for further preening of its feathers. It is also vital that your Grey's diet includes food rich in calcium and Vitamin D.

Aspergillosis

It is a respiratory disease caused by the fungus called *Aspergillus*, which is found in warm and moist environments.

a.) Cause and Effect

The microscopic spores of Aspergillus are an airborne transmitted disease. The fungus does not cause the disease per se but if your bird does not have a healthy immune system it can cause illness.

It increases the chances of the spores being inhaled by your bird if the environment has poor ventilation and sanitation, dusty conditions, and in close confinements.

Other predisposing factors include poor nutrition, other medical conditions in the respiratory system and prolonged use of antibiotics or corticosteroids, which eventually weakens the immune system. Aspergillosis is more common in parrots than other pet birds.

b.) Signs and Symptoms

There are two kinds of Aspergillosis, it's either acute or chronic, both of which attacks the respiratory system.

Acute Aspergillosis signs and symptoms include:

- Severe difficulty in breathing
- Cyanosis (a bluish coloration of mucous membranes and/or skin)
- Decreased or loss of appetite
- Frequent drinking and urination

Chronic Aspergillosis symptoms include:

- White nodules appear through the respiratory tissue
- Large numbers of spores enter the bloodstream
- Infection in the kidneys, skin, muscle, gastrointestinal tract, liver, eyes, and brain

Other signs of Aspergillosis may include:

- Rapid breathing
- Exercise intolerance
- Change in syrinx (voice box); reluctance to talk
- Discharged and clogging of Nares
- Tremors

- Seizures or paralysis
- Green discoloration in the urates may be seen
- Enlarged liver
- Gout (painful, inflamed joints due to urate deposits)
- Depression and lethargy

c.) Diagnosis of Aspergillosis

Aspergillosis is generally difficult to detect until complete diagnosis. Do not compromise respiratory infections, consult the veterinarian immediately.
Here are some of the tests that your African Grey needs to undergo through for diagnosis

- Radiographs (a complete blood count)
- Endoscopy (used to view lesions in the syrinx or trachea)
- PCR testing for the presence of Aspergillus

d.) Treatment and Remedy

Always consult a veterinarian first to know the right remedy for your bird. There are reports that the antifungal drug Itraconazole may be more toxic to African grey parrots than to other bird species. Another antifungal drug called Amphotericin B may be administered orally, topically, by injection, or nebulizing. Consult your vet for proper guidance. Surgery may also be performed to remove accessible lesions. Supportive care is often needed such as oxygen, supplemental heat, tube feeding, and treatment of underlying conditions.

e.) Prevention

Maintaining a good husbandry and diet can highly prevent outbreaks of Aspergillosis.

Below are some tips you can do to ensure that your bird is free from such a deadly disease:

- Keep your bird in a well-ventilated environment.
- Always clean the food and water dishes
- Thoroughly clean cages, toys, perches and other accessories at least once a month.
- Replace substrate (material lining the cage bottom) regularly
- Offer a good nutrition, such as the right combination of fruits, vegetables and seeds

Psittacine Beak and Feather Disease (PBFD)

PBFD is a viral condition that is responsible for damage to the beak, feathers and nails as well as the immune system of infected birds. These are very common in African grey parrots between 6 months and 3 years of age.

a.) Signs and symptoms

PBFD typically affects the feathers of infected birds as well as its beak and nails over time. Here are some signs and symptoms that your pet might have PBFD.

- Feathers are short, fragile, malformed, and prone to bleeding and breaking. Birds may first lose their the white, fine powder produced by specialized feathers to help maintain feather health when this happens more abnormal feathers will eventually develop.
- Beak has become glossy rather than the more typical matte appearance
- Nails and beak becomes brittle and malformed
- Significant loss of feathers (as the follicles become damaged)
- Loss of appetite (especially in young Greys)
- Regurgitation or continuous vomiting

b.) Diagnosis

Veterinarians will likely perform a PCR test to confirm the diagnosis. This test uses advanced techniques to look for the virus' DNA.

Most of the time PCR only needs a blood sample, but your veterinarian may also need to take a swab from your bird's mouth and vent.

Other kinds of test may include:

- Complete blood count and a chemistry panel tests.
- DNA test for specifically for PBFD

c.) Treatment

The majority of clinically affected birds will die within a few months to a year because there are no antiviral drugs available to fight the virus. Your avian veterinarian can only help keep your bird comfortable because this condition is painful for the bird and it also allows secondary infections to take hold. Some birds may survive for a few months they will ultimately die from this disease.

d.) Prevention

The only thing breeders and pet owners can do to prevent this deadly virus is to take pro-active steps but since you can't help the birds mingle with other birds as they travel from wholesaler to retail pet distributors to your home the best solution is to have your bird examined by an avian veterinarian and allow diagnostic testing.

It is also wise to take your bird for a yearly exam to make sure it stays healthy. Yearly exams can catch small issues before they get worse.

2.) Signs of Possible Illnesses

For you to keep your African Greys healthy, you need to monitor them to ensure that they are in good condition, however there will come a time that your bird will get sick. Here are some early warning signs that your Grey could be potentially ill.

- **Activity** – Is your bird sleeping when it normally does not? Or being quiet when it normally isn't? Is there a decreased in food and water intake or not being able to eat at all like before?
- **Droppings** (feces) - Are there any change in urates (white part) or feces that is lasting more than 1-2 days?
- **Diarrhea** - Have you found undigested food in your bird's feces? Their droppings should have the three distinct parts (green/brown, white and liquid urine). If you think your grey has diarrhea, contact your vet immediately.
- **Weight loss** - Does your bird feels "light" when you pick it up? That maybe a sign of weight loss because the Keel bone becomes more prominent.
- **Feathers** – Is there a continuous presence of pinfeathers? It may be dull in color, broken, bent and fluffed up feathers.
- **Sneezing** – Is there a discharge in the nostrils when

your bird sneezes? Look for stained feathers over the nares or crusty material in or around the nostrils.

- **Vomiting** – Has your pet been vomiting for quite a long period of time already? Greys and all birds regurgitate as a sign of "affection" but it could also indicate a crop infection

- **Respiratory** – Are there signs of respiratory distress like tail bobbing up and down with each breath, a change in breathing sounds, and wheezing or clicking noise when it inhales?

- **Balance** – Has your bird been falling off its perch and huddling at the bottom of cage? It is a sign that it's losing its balance.

- **Eyes** – Does it appear dull? Is there a redness/swelling and loss of feathers around the eyes?

- **Feet** – Is it scaly or flaky? Does it have sores on the bottom of the feet?

- **Head** – Have you noticed excessive head bobbing and shaking?

When these things happen, contact your avian veterinarian immediately. Do not compromise your bird's health; prevention is always better than cure.

Chapter Eight: African Grey Checklist

Congratulate yourself! You are now on your way to becoming a very well-informed and pro-active African Grey owner! Finishing this book is a huge milestone for you and your future or present pet bird, but before this ultimate guide comes to a conclusion, keep in mind the most important things you have acquired through reading this book. This chapter will outline the summary of you what you have learned, the do's and dont's as well as the checklist you need to tick off to ensure that you and your African Greys lived happily ever after!

1.) Basic Information

- **Taxonomy**: phylum *Chordata*, class *Aves*, order *Psittaciformes*, family *Psittacidae*, Genus *Psittacus*, Species *Psittacus Erithacus*
- **Distribution**: Kenya, Ivory Coast, Guinea-Bissau, Sierra Leone, Ghana
- **Habitat**: Tropical; Terrestrial
- **Anatomical Adaptations**:
- **Eggs**: 3 to 5 eggs per season
- **Incubation Period**: 30 days
- **Average Size**: 33 cm from head to tail
- **Average Weight**: 407 grams
- **Wingspan**: 46 – 52 cm
- **Coloration**: White face patches, Grey contour feathers, black beaks, red tails, silvery yellow eyes
- **Sexual Dimorphism**: Males are slightly longer than females; Females have a narrower head and a suppler neck.
- **Diet**: nuts, fruits, seeds, insects, flowers
- **Vocalization**: mimicry; choruses
- **Lifespan**: 23 years in the wild; 45 to 60 years in captivity

2.) Cage Set-up Guide

- **Minimum Cage Dimensions**: 2 feet deep by 3 feet wide by 4 feet high (61 x 91 x 122 cm) for single bird; 2 feet width, 3 feet high & 6 feet deep during breeding period.
- **Cage Shape**: the bigger, the better. Never purchase a round cage.
- **Minimum Height**: 48 inches (121 cm)
- **Bar Spacing**: ¾ to 1 inch
- **Required Accessories**: food and water dishes, perches, grooming and cleaning materials, cuttlebone, toys
- **Food/Water Dish**: 3 sturdy dishes; one for fresh water, one for pellet/seed mix, and one for fresh foods.
- **Perches**: at least 3 different perches; wood dowel, natural branch type, a therapeutic perch or a cement perch
- **Recommended Toys**: rotate at least 3 different toys; rope toys, stainless steel bells, swings etc.
- **Bathing Materials**: misting bottle; bath tub
- **Nests**: made from wood or bamboo
- **Nesting Materials**: soft wood shavings and small twigs
- **Recommended Temperature Range**: average temperature, it should not exceed 80 degrees.
- **Lighting:** full color light bulb must be present in the cage area

3.) Nutritional Information

- **Diet in Captivity**: 5-10% of an African grey's diet should be bite-sized
- **Types of Recommended Food:**
- **Seeds:** 3-4 teaspoons per day
- **Fresh Fruits and Vegetables:** About 5-10% of an African grey's diet should be bite-sized. Offer fruits and vegetables daily or every 2-3 days.
- **Supplements:** Calcium usually found in the form of a cuttlebone or Calcium treat. Powdered supplement such as packaged oyster shell can be added directly to your pet's food.
- **Vitamins:** recommended food rich in Vitamin A approved by your veterinarian.
- **Water:** clean, fresh and cool water; unflavored bottled drinking water or bottled natural spring water

4.) Breeding Tips

- **Sexual Dimorphism**: only determined through DNA analysis. DNA testing can also determine the sexual maturity and capability to reproduce.
- **Seasonal Changes**: mating season usually begins in October or during dry season and egg laying in November.

- **Mating Behavior:** takes place between midnight and around four o'clock in the morning. They mate for almost 20 minutes.
- **Nest Size:** an L shaped nest that measures 2 feet high and two feet deep at the base.
- **Egg Laying**: female lays lay 4-5 eggs with a gap of 2-3 days per season
- **Clutch Size**: 4 to 5 eggs per clutch
- **Incubation Period**: 30 days on average
- **Hatching**: takes about 28-30 days to hatch

5.) Do's and Dont's

- Do feed them a variety of nutritious food
- Do train them well to maximize their intelligence
- Do provide a clean and healthy environment
- Do give them time and commitment
- Do care for them when they feel ill
- Do bond with them and let them out of the cage once in a while so that they can be exposed outside
- Do not use sandpaper covered perches or floor paper. It can cause severe damage to your bird's feet
- Do not use "bird disks" or "mite disks". These may harm your bird. See your avian veterinarian if you suspect parasites.

- Do not use bird gravel. Bird gravel is used for birds that do not crack the hull or shell of the seeds they eat. It causes severe impactions, which are often fatal. Gravel only benefits doves and pigeons definitely not parrots
- Do not use negative reinforcement during training because it is not effective
- Don't let African Greys fall. It may contribute in developing respiratory problems and damages organs due to impact. Teach them how to fly!

Chapter Nine: Relevant Websites

Finishing this book doesn't mean that you should stop learning! This chapter provides you a wealth of references online that you could check out every now and then so that you can be updated when it comes to taking care of your African Grey parrot. You can also find the websites you need to visit especially in buying cages and supplies for your pet.

1. *African Grey Cage Links*

Here is the recommended list of websites for you to choose from when buying cages both in United States and Great Britain.

United States Links:

Cages by Design

<http://www.cagesbydesign.com/t-AfricanGreyCages.aspx>

Bird Cages 4 Less

<http://birdcages4less.com/page/B/CTGY/African-Grey-Bird-Cages>

Bird Cages Now

<http://www.birdcagesnow.com/african-greys/>

King's Cages

<http://www.kingscages.com/SearchResults.aspx?CategoryID=Cages>

Pet Solutions

<http://www.petsolutions.com/C/Large-Bird-Cages-Greys-Amazons-Sm-Cockatoos.aspx>

Great Britain Links:

Cages World

<http://www.cagesworld.co.uk/f/Parrot_Cages/products::bird_type:African_Grey.htm>

Northern Parrots

<http://www.northernparrots.com/african-grey-cages-deptb101147/>

Pebble – Home and Garden

<https://www.pebble.co.uk/compare.html?q=African-Grey-Cages-Sale>

Seapets

<https://www.seapets.co.uk/bird-supplies/bird-cages/parrot-cages>

2. *African Grey Cage Accessories*

Here is the recommended list of websites for you to choose from when buying accessories such as toys, perches, dishes and other necessary supplies for your pet.

United States Links:

Fun Time Birdy - Toys

<http://www.funtimebirdy.com/largebirdtoys.html>

Northern Parrots - Toys

< http://www.northernparrots.com/african-grey-accessories-deptb101146/>

PetSmart – Perches and Accessories

<http://www.petsmart.com/bird/toys-perches-decor/cat-36-catid-400010>

Wind City Parrot - Accessories

<http://www.windycityparrot.com/African-Grey_c_606.html>

Great Britain Links:

Cages World - Accessories
<http://www.cagesworld.co.uk/c/Bird_Cage_Accessories.ht
m>

Parrot Essentials - Accessories

<http://www.parrotessentials.co.uk/>

Parrotize UK – Parrot Stands and Covers

<http://parrotize.co.uk/products/parrot-stands/>

Seapets – Bird Toys

<https://www.seapets.co.uk/bird-supplies/bird-toys>

ZooPlus – Accessories
<http://www.zooplus.co.uk/shop/birds/cage_accessories>

3. African Grey Diet and Food Links

Here is the recommended list of websites for you to choose from when buying seeds and parrot food for your pet.

United States Links:

Harrison's Bird Food

<http://www.harrisonsbirdfoods.com/>

Pet Supplies Plus

<http://www.petsuppliesplus.com/thumbnail/Bird/Food-Treats/c/2142/2162.uts>

Weluma

<http://us.weluma.com/search/?q=African+Grey+Pellets&source=searchbar>

Wind City Parrot

<http://www.windycityparrot.com/African-Grey_c_606.html>

Great Britain Links:

Northern Parrots – African Grey Supplements

<http://www.northernparrots.com/african-grey-supplements-deptb101187/>

Scarletts Parrot Essentials UK - African Grey feeds

<https://www.scarlettsparrotessentials.co.uk/catalogsearch/advanced/result/?name=African+Grey&x=0&y=0>

Seapets – African Grey Treats, Bird Food

<https://www.seapets.co.uk/bird-supplies/bird-toys/parrot-treats>

ZooPlus – African Grey Food

<http://www.zooplus.com/shop/birds/bird_food/parrot>

Index

A

accessories 14,15,16,63,70,77,78
activity 15,66
african grey......2,3,4,5,6,7,8,9,11,12,13,14,15,16,17,18,19,20,21,22,23,24,25,
    27,29,30,32,33,34,35,38,39,40,41,42,43,44,45,46,47,48,51,52,53,54,55,57,5
    8,62,64,66,68,71,73,74
animal movement license.. 22
Aspergillosis 60,61,62,63
Avian Veterinary.. 44
Aviary.. 26,27,28

B

baby 14,29,49,55,58
beak 6,9,36,37,59,63,64,69
behavior... 12,13,14,47,52,72
bird bath 36
bite-sized 42,71
bond.. 46,54,72
breeder 19,23,24,25,26,27,30,52,65
breeding.. 4,5,51,52,53,54,70,71
brooding... 55

C

cage..13,14,15,16,18,20,33,34,35,3
    7,42,45,47,53,54,55,63,67,70,72,74,75,76, 77,78
calcium... 13,35,42,43,58,59,60,71
captivity 5,6,55,69,71
care... 5,14,16,17,18,30,32,36,37,43,63,72,74
causes 57,73

chick.. 54,59

CITES...20,21

cleaning..16,17,18,70

clutch 5,24,72

color..5,8,9,37,66,70

coloration..6,61,62,69

conditions 21,33,43,60,63

cost 11,12,14,15,16,17,18,60

cyanosis...61

cuttlebone..35,42,70,71

D

diagnosis 62,64

diet....................................6,13,17,24,35,38,39,42,43,60,63,69,71,79

diseases...22,39,43,54,57,58,59

dishes..15,35,63,70,77

DNA..52,64,65,71

droppings 66

E

eggs...5,6,43,53,54,55,59,69,71,72

egg Binding 59

environment 14,33,54,55,60,63,72

eyes..3,6,30,61,67,69

F

family 6,14,43,69

feather 66,67,69

Feather Loss 64

feeding..15,17,38,40,42,63

female...................................3,6,51,52,53,54,55,69,72

flap...47

fly..45,46,48,73
follicle 64
food 16,17,18,33,35,38,39,4244,55,60,63,66,70,71,72,79,80
fruits 3,5,6,17,39,41,42,43,44,63,69,71

G

genus 6,69
grooming..14,16,36,70

H

habitat 6,33,38,69
handling 36,45
hatching 55,72
health... 24,33,35,58,59,64,67
healthy.......................................17,19,30,32,33,36,38,39,41,54,57,60,65,66,72
history.. 7
husbandry 63
hygiene 16,36
hypocalceamia..58

I

illness 60,64
immune system..40,43,59,60,61
incubation 5,6,55,69,72
infection...61,62,63,64,65,67
initial costs 14,16
insects..5,6,69
impact..12,73
impactions..73

L

lay...5,53,54,55,72
laying...71,72
lesions..62,63
license... 22
lifespan..5,6,69
longevity...30

M

maneuver... 47
male.. 6,51,52,53,54,69
mandibles 3
mating...53,71,72
maturity 52,71
mites 72

N

nails 36,46,48,63,64
nares...61,67
nest.. 4, 5,54,55,70,72
nesting 70
nesting materials... 70
nutrients 39
nutritional..17,38,39,71
needs 12,15,16,17,32,34,35,39,62,64

O

oil...36
oil-palm...3,5
order...5

P

pair... 5,54
parents... 5,55
parrots...4,5,7,8,12,14,15,35,37,38,39,41,42,43,4
4,48,52,53,54,58,59,60,62,64,73
PBFD virus...63,64,65
pellet... 17,35,39,43,70
perches 15,33,35,47,48,63,70,72,77
permit 21,22
personality 12
pet store 16,17,23,24
plants 20,44
population... 20
prevention...22,57,59,63,65,67
pros and cons 11,12

Q

quarantine 3
quick 6,46

R

Red Tail 6,9,69
reproduction 4,52,53,54
regurgitation...64,67
respiratory..36,60,61,62,67,73

S

season...4,6,69,71,72
seed mix... 35,70
seeds...36,17,35,39,63,69,70,71,73,79

sexing..52

sexually dimorphism 6,52,69,71

species 3,4,5,6,12,13,15,20,21,62,69

styptic powder 48

symptoms 57,58,59,61,64

T

tail...3,4,6,9,67,69

temperature...37,70

terrestrial 5,6,69

toys 14,15,16,18,35,63,70,77

training...............................14,17,45,46,47,72,73

treatment.............................17,44,58,59,62,63,65

type..8,15,16,39,71

U

United States.................................. 5,20,21,22,23,25,75

V

vegetables...17,39,40,42,44,63,71

ventilation 60

veterinarian...............36,41,43,49,54,59,62,64,65,67,71,72

virus 64,65

W

water 17,35,36,43,44,63,66,70,71

wild 5,6,20,21,48,54,55,69

wingspan...4,6

Photo Credits

Page 1 Photo by Flickr user karolyn83, <https://pixabay.com/en/grey-parrot-african-grey-parrot-1140551/>

Page 2 Photo By Flickr user Avenue, <https://commons.wikimedia.org/wiki/File:African_Grey_Parrot,_peeking_out_from_under_its_wing.jpg>

Page 4 Photo By Flickr user Keith Allison, <https://www.flickr.com/photos/keithallison/3894381786/>

Page 8 Photo By Administrator <http://www.africangreyparrot.org/african-grey-parrots/>

Page 11 Photo By Flickr user Keith Allison, <https://www.flickr.com/photos/keithallison/3894381384/in/photostream/>

Page 13 Photo By bobistraveling via Wikimedia Commons, <https://commons.wikimedia.org/wiki/File:African_Grey_Parrots_Sylvan_Heights_Waterfowl_Park.jpg>

Page 68 Photo By Sandy Cole via Wikimedia Commons <https://commons.wikimedia.org/wiki/File:African_Grey_Parrot_SMTC.jpg>

Page 74 Photo By Flickr user Keith Allison, <https://www.flickr.com/photos/keithallison/3714139147>

References

"African Grey Cage and Environment."
African-Grey-Parrot.com
<http://www.african-grey-parrot.com/Housing-And-
Cages.aspx>

"African Grey Diseases." BeautyofBirds.com
<https://www.beautyofbirds.com/africangreydiseases.html>

"African Grey Facts and FAQs." AfricanGreyParrot.org
<http://www.africangreyparrot.org/african-grey-parrots-
facts-faqs/>

"African Grey Facts and Info." African-Grey-Parrot.net
<http://www.african-grey-parrot.net/>

"African Grey in General." AfricanGreyParrot.org
<http://www.africangreyparrot.org/>

"African Grey Health." African-Grey-Parrot.com
<http://www.african-grey-parrot.com/African-Grey-
Health.aspx>

"African Grey in History." AlexFoundation.org
<http://alexfoundation.org/the-birds/alex/>
"All About African Grey." African-Grey.com

<http://african-grey.com/home/>

"African Grey Parrot." Lafeber.com
<https://lafeber.com/pet-birds/species/african-grey-parrot/>

"African Grey Parrot Taxonomy." AquaticCommunity.com
<http://www.aquaticcommunity.com/africangrey/>

"African Grey Permit." BirdTricks.com
<http://www.birdtricks.com/African_Grey_Parrot_and_CITE
S_Permit.htm>

"Breeding African Gray Parrots." AfricanGreyParrots.net
<http://www.africangreyparrots.net/breeding-african-gray-
parrots/>

"Congo and Timneh African grey."
African-Grey-Parrot.com
<http://www.african-grey-parrot.com/>

"Do's and Dont's for African Grey parrot."
BirdChannel.com
<http://www.birdchannel.com/bird-species/find-the-right-
bird/african-grey-dos-and-donts.aspx>

"How to Breed African Greys." Bluequaker.com

<http://www.bluequaker.com/Art-006.htm>

"How to Train African Greys." TrainedParrot.com
http://trainedparrot.com/Taming/

"Psittacus erithacus, Grey Parrot." BirdLife International
<http://www.iucnredlist.org/pdflink.48141088>

"Psittacus erithacus, African Grey." AnimalDivesity.org
<http://animaldiversity.org/accounts/Psittacus_erithacus/>

"Signs and Illnesses of African Grey Parrots."
African-Grey-Parrot.com
<http://www.african-grey-parrot.com/African-Grey-Illness-
    Signs.aspx"

"Top 10 Pet African Grey Parrot Questions Answered."
BirdChannel.com
<http://www.birdchannel.com/bird-species/find-the-right-
bird/pet-african-grey-faq.aspx>

Feeding Baby
Cynthia Cherry
978-1941070000

Axolotl
Lolly Brown
978-0989658430

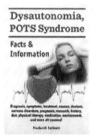

Dysautonomia, POTS
Syndrome
Frederick Earlstein
978-0989658485

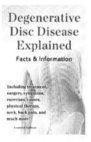

Degenerative Disc
Disease Explained
Frederick Earlstein
978-0989658485

Sinusitis, Hay Fever,
Allergic Rhinitis Explained
Frederick Earlstein
978-1941070024

Wicca
Riley Star
978-1941070130

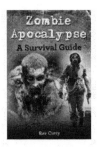

Zombie Apocalypse
Rex Cutty
978-1941070154

Capybara
Lolly Brown
978-1941070062

Eels As Pets
Lolly Brown
978-1941070167

Scabies and Lice Explained
Frederick Earlstein
978-1941070017

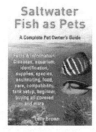

Saltwater Fish As Pets
Lolly Brown
978-0989658461

Torticollis Explained
Frederick Earlstein
978-1941070055

Kennel Cough
Lolly Brown
978-0989658409

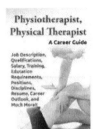

Physiotherapist, Physical
Therapist
Christopher Wright
978-0989658492

Rats, Mice, and Dormice
As Pets
Lolly Brown
978-1941070079

Wallaby and Wallaroo Care
Lolly Brown
978-1941070031

Bodybuilding Supplements
Explained
Jon Shelton
978-1941070239

Demonology
Riley Star
978-19401070314

Pigeon Racing
Lolly Brown
978-1941070307

Dwarf Hamster
Lolly Brown
978-1941070390

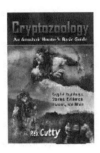

Cryptozoology
Rex Cutty
978-1941070406

Eye Strain
Frederick Earlstein
978-1941070369

Inez The Miniature Elephant
Asher Ray
978-1941070353

Vampire Apocalypse
Rex Cutty
978-1941070321

Printed in Great Britain
by Amazon

55453414R00063